# Learn How To Make Money
## With Your eBay And PayPal Account Now

By Morgan Johnson

Kindle Edition

## TABLE OF CONTENTS

·Copyright Info
·Foreward
·Intro
·Chapter 1 EASY MONEY IN YOUR EBAY AND PAYPAL ACCOUNT
·Chapter 2 LET'S FACE IT, ELECTRONICS ARE IN DEMAND
·Chapter 3 HEY, WHAT'S THE BIG IDEA
·Chapter 4 THINGS YOU WILL NEED
·Chapter 5 THE STEPS TO TAKE
·Chapter 6 RECOMMENDED EMAIL OPERATIONS ACCOUNT
·Chapter 7 THE DEBIT CARD THAT YOU USE
·Chapter 8 SETUP ACCOUNTS WITH YOUR PRODUCT SOURCE COMPANY(S)
·Chapter 9 HOW TO OPERATE THIS SYSTEM
·Chapter 10 USING YOUR EBAY AND PAYPAL ACCOUNT
·Chapter 11 MAKING MONEY ONLINE IN NO TIME FLAT
·Chapter 12 HOW TO SET YOUR PROFIT MARGIN
·Chapter 13 WHERE THE MAGIC HAPPENS
·Chapter 14 DO THIS AND MAKE MONEY
·Chapter 15 OUR UNIQUE LIST OF PRODUCT SOURCE COMPANIES
·About the Author
·Special Bonus Offer
**Book Description**

# COPYRIGHT INFORMATION

**Learn How To Make Money With Your eBay And PayPal Account Now**
Copyright 2012-2016 Morgan Johnson

All rights reserved World Wide.

MoJohnson Publishing
Model: ISBN-13
Product ID: 4154486
ISBN-13: 978-1482326352 (CreateSpace-Assigned)
ISBN-10: 1482326353
BISAC: Business & Economics / Home-based Businesses

Score is 9 out of 10 based on 10 reviews

# Foreword

To know the person that wrote this mini e-book is to know humanity.
It is because of his humanity that the Author felt that he should share his knowledge about making money online.

Most of you who will read this mini e-book would never guess how easy it is to make money online. So this e-book was written to get this message out to all who were looking for a better and easier way to supplement their income or just wanted to make an income period. With all the trouble of today's world economy, and the slowing job market here in America, more and more people are looking for alternate ways to make money to live a better life and be able to provide for their families.

This book was written out of pure passion and desire to help eradicate poverty and to broadcast a message for those looking for an easy way to make money. It was my goal that this e-book could be used as a tool to help people start their own home based business. I'm sure that after reading it anyone could learn to harness the power of the internet and begin to generate an independent income to help them selves out of poverty.

This mini e-book has great information that some of the big corporate elites would not want you to know.

The reason why the Author took it upon himself to write this book is because this mini e-book could set **YOU** on the path to financial independence.

There were many that stood in his way denied him opportunity, so it was with the writing of this mini-e-book tutorial that he would defy all oppressors and opportunity it's self would be held hostage no more.

**Free enterprise once again for all to obtain!**

# Intro
## "This is a quick study mini eBook"

**READ this eBook** as it will explain how to easily start making money online with your eBay and PayPal Account.

This eBook will tell you how to make money online with $0.00 dollar start-up cost and all within 48-to-72 hours after setup.

<u>LEARN HOW TO MAKE MONEY WITH YOUR EBAY AND PAYPAL ACCOUNT NOW</u>

# Chapter 1
## "EASY MONEY WITH YOUR EBAY AND PAYPAL ACCOUNT"

## GOT AN EBAY AND PAYPAL ACCOUNT WITH NO MONEY IN THEM?

**THEN LISTEN UP!**

Learn how to make money with your eBay and PayPal account fast and easy!

Start making money online right now with this simple no money startup cost system.

You don't need your own website to do this but you can if you want to.

You don't need to sell your old or unwanted items from your garage or some creepy old dress left hanging in you're spooked out attic.

You just simply need to learn an easy way to sell other peoples products and like magic make a nice commission in the middle. The up side of this is that all of these products will be brand named and brand new in the box shipped directly from the manufacturer or authorized dealer right to the front door step of your customer.

With this great system that you are about to learn it's suggested to see more profit more quickly that you get into a fast moving high volume market niche like consumer electronics. Home and mobile electronic are some of the fastest moving items on the internet. And don't misunderstand me here.., when I say fastest moving.., I mean some of the fastest selling items on the web are electronics.

**NOTE TO READER:**
THIS METHOD CAN ALSO BE APPLIED TO ALMOST ANY PRODUCTS THAT YOU CHOOSE TO SELL ONLINE!

## Chapter 2
### "LETS FACE IT ELECTRONICS ARE IN DEMAND"

**NOW WITH THAT SAID:**

If you do a little research you will find that people are always buying and selling electronics online. And if you haven't guessed it by now, selling high end home and mobile electronics and the accessories also always make for as better commission when selling online.

Selling online via the internet is easier faster and customer approved. It's just really convenient for everybody involved. The buyer doesn't have to spend the time to go to the physical store and begin to look to shop are for what think they are looking for and then ask themselves what do I want to buy., which I might add is also a great time saver right there. Because when you get right down to it where the rubber meets the road, time is money! Well the point of all of that is when shopping online it's just more convenient because first you don't have to look for what you want because there it is right on your computer screen and now all you have to do is point and click the buy now button and your done. Okay, okay, okay there is one little drawback when shopping online, and that is that you have to wait a few days before you receive your product purchase. In my opinion, it's not a bad trade off. If you have been paying attention to innovation.., Amazon has got that aspect licked. They now have fling drones that deliver your products to your door step. And I know you've got to be saying.., "You got to be kidding me" and I'd be like…, "I kid you not!" They take your order and if your deliver address is within distance they will fly your purchase item out to your house. They have same day service, FAA license and everything!

If there's any buying and selling going on–on the internet.., then it's most definitely happening on eBay and Amazon. These are the best two places outside of Google to be selling online period. I have to say and you must be made aware that eBay and Amazon really have the buying and selling platforms of the whole internet in there back pockets. Currently and what seems to be for the foreseeable future.., that games belongs to them.

**STATISTICS SHOW THAT AT ANY GIVEN TIME DURING THE DAY OVER HALF THE WORLD'S INTERNET TRAFFIC IS ON EITHER EBAY, OR AMAZON.**

These are the places on the internet that most people in the world with internet access are going to buy and sell online or bid and trade online.

In essence, on the internet…, Amazon and eBay is where the money is. And the message here for this chapter is that..,

**IF YOU ARE GOING TO SELL ONLINE, GO WHERE THE MONEY IS!**

# Chapter 3
## "HEY, WHAT'S THE BIG IDEA"

**The question that everyone seems to be asking here lately is:**

Can you really start making money online with no money to startup at all?
Drum roll please!
And the answer is,
**YES!**

You just need to know how to use the right free tools offered online and know the right free places to set up your accounts to start doing so.

Be to the wiser. There is no secret way to make money online. It's only a secret because no one has told you how to do it.


**Learn this method, work this plan, make my system your system and you will beat your competition to the sell every time and begin to put money into your PayPal account fast and easy.**

# Chapter 4
## "THINGS YOU WILL NEED"

**The accounts you will need for this system are listed below:**
PayPal Account (Free to Setup)
eBay Account (Free to Setup)
Bank Account (Free to Setup +Your Deposit)

**NOTE:**
As an independent sales merchant you can expand your sells platform from not just using eBay but also start selling on Amazon, Craig's List, use classified ads, bid and auction sites, and also you can set up product data feeds to have all of your store items inserted into the digital market place to increase your product visibility to online customers and in turn increase your sales and profits.

The more active sell platforms you sign up with the better! This way you get more exposure for your products and the more exposure you get means the more products you can sell.

**IMPORTANT:**
Please understand that with this system you are basically becoming a middleman. In this context and your use of this system you are connecting the person or client that wants to buy with the person or client that wants to sell.

You are just the go between and inadvertently you get paid in the middle. In the middle means that you were the connecting factor within the transaction that made the buy ands sell possible. It is for this service that you are entitled to make your commission. Let No one tell you different, because we freelance around here where I'm from!

When you first begin you have to tweak the system to what best fits you and your scale for profits. So we went a little farther to help you with your mission to be independent and in this business in regards to your profit every cent counts.

Don't play with your money and your money won't play with you!

**WE ALSO TELL YOU HOW TO SET YOUR PROFIT MARGIN BUT FOR NOW JUST READ ON!**

# Chapter 5
## "THE STEPS TO TAKE"

**FIRST:**

#1.

If you don't have a bank account with a debit card attached to it, we suggest getting a prepaid debt card from your local Ace Check Cashing, or a Rush Card or something of the like. These prepaid debit cards usually have a virtual bank account with an account number and routing number attached to you prepaid debit card.

You can then use this information to completely setup your PayPal, eBay, Amazon, and or data feed accounts to begin to get your product items out in front of your online customers. Make no mistake.., these are not just mere accounts, these are your tools that you use online to make sales, ship items and transfer money.

The reason for the above is obviously to ensure that you have an account setup, established and attached so that you can have a place to deposit the profits from your commission into your bank account at the end of the day.

**IMPORTANT:**

Do not use your PayPal Business debit card to make personal transactions. You generally only want to use your PayPal business debit cards to make business purchases. I think that's also kind of why the have you attach your personal bank account to your PayPal account so that you can transfer funds that you plan to use for personal reasons into your personal bank account. I think that way it gives the opportunity not to mix your apples with your oranges so to speak.

Okay.., are you having fun yet?
If so keep reading…

# Chapter 6
## "RECOMMENDED EMAIL OPERATIONS ACCOUNT"

**NEXT:**

#2.

(Recommended)

If you don't have one setup, we recommend that you take some time out to setup a new gmail account with Google.

Try and set the user name to something like a shop for the type of items that you will be selling.

**EXAMPLE:**  mycoolelectronicsshop@gmail.com

Once it is setup, use your new gmail account to setup your new PayPal, eBay, Amazon, Classified Ads, and Data Feed Accounts.

(All of which are optional and free to setup)

**IMPORTANT:**

When setting up your PayPal Account:

Attach and connect your bank account or your prepaid debit card account to your PayPal account so that you can then transfer your profits into your bank account which when done correctly it will make for much better use and record at tax time.

# Chapter 7
## "THE DEBIT CARD THAT YOU USE"

After you setup your PayPal account, apply for and receive your PayPal debit card. (Free to apply)

Your PayPal debit card will usually be sent to you and arrive in the mail in about 2 weeks from your application request with PayPal.

This will be the debit card you use to make all business purchase transactions with your product item suppliers.

You will and should only purchase your customer orders with your PayPal business debit card. This means setup all of your supplier accounts using this PayPal debit card to make purchase from them.

YOU ONLY BUY WHEN YOU RECEIVE CONFORMATION EMAIL OF PRODUCT SOLD.

**IMPORTANT:**
When you receive your PayPal debit card remember to keep it safe. This will be the debit card that you use to buy the products that have already been pre-sold in your eBay, Amazon, Google merchant account or the like.

**NEXT**
#3.
Set up an eBay/Amazon/Craig's List, and Classified Ads Account: (Free)
Beginning with your eBay/Amazon/Craig's List, and Classified Ads Account, you can use these accounts to list, post, and sell your products online.

**REMEMBER:**
All of your eBay/Amazon/Craig's List and Classified Ads Accounts are only created to facilitate the sell.

Your eBay/Amazon/Craig's List and Classified Ads Account are all online buying and selling platforms and there are many, many more like them but eBay and Amazon as earlier stated.., they have this market cornered.

The online platforms named above are in which the ones you would like to have your product items listed for sale. Hands down and no doubt about it!

**NOTE:**
You should almost never buy from the sites above to supply your customer. Buying for personal reasons is okay but not for your customer. Always do research to find the best suppliers outside of eBay and Amazon for the product items you sell online. You should only buy from where you sell if there is only no alternative or if you just can't pass up on beating the profit margin that you can make with the better deal that you have found on the site where you are selling from some guy/gal with a much better deal than yours. There is a balance that must be adhered to here people!

.

# Chapter 8
## "SETUP ACCOUNTS WITH YOUR PRODUCT SOURCE COMPANY(S)"

**NEXT**
#4.
This system gives you our go to sources to find the high profit products to sell online at the end of the little tutorial.

Setup and establish relationships and transaction accounts with the product sourcing companies that we will provide to you below.

**(All accounts are free to setup)**

**NOTE:**
With some source accounts with the provided suppliers below, you will be required to send in a copy of your Photo ID, and a W-9 Tax Information for your account registration and setup.

When this is done you will become somewhat of a reseller/distributor for the products that you sell trough your product source/supplier company account(s).

**ALSO:**
Some may require a business tax ID number and some will allow you to use just your personal social security number. It just depends on which you choose to use in your business endeavor.

With the sources that we name below, once you set up your merchant account with them, you can find high end name brand consumer home and mobile electronics from 20%-50% off the MRSV price..

This way you can begin to find and buy name brand electronics at greatly reduced prices.

This ultimately means that you can leverage this insider product access to buy low and sell high!

Please don't make this into rocket science! Because it's not! It's easy!

**IT'S REALLY EASY!**
Follow these methods and the products are pre-sold before you buy to them sell. This way you always get to set what type of profit you are making before the whole of the transaction takes place.

**IN OTHER WORDS,**
All that I'm saying here to you is that you won't have to buy from your supplier source until the product is pre-sold; the money is in your PayPal account, and it has been made available for your immediate use.

It just doesn't get any easier than this!

# Chapter 9
## "HOW TO OPERATE THIS SYSTEM"

**HOW THIS OPERATES:**
After all your accounts have been setup and you have your debit card(s) in place in hand, you are ready to rock and roll.

Begin by posting your chosen product line listing on your chosen product selling platforms like eBay/Amazon/Classified Ads site to begin your selling.

**RECOMMENDATIONS:**
When posting products on eBay, I recommend posting no more than 10 products at a time and the same goes for Amazon if you choose to use them. The reason for this is that things can get to be pretty complicated with all of the requirements of product attributes and the like. This can relate into hard work if you let it. You have to plan your work and work your plan and not let it work you.

As a rule of thumb, only buy and post new products to sell to your customers.

Always post at buy now prices and do not use the auction feature with eBay or otherwise unless you have taken this method strictly as your business model.

Another tip you can use is that when looking for products to list and sell online, try and search only for the products that you would like to sell that has a free shipping label attached to it within your supplier account(s). This makes for greater profits in the end!

**NOTE:**
Did you know that you can also create buy now buttons from within your PayPal account to attach to your product listing that you may have on your own website if you have one? And if you have one you should make sure that it's getting great traffic. Or you can just skip all of that and go to the source of where the money is as stated earlier if you missed it.

That's the beauty of eBay and Amazon, the TRAFFIC and the MONEY is already there!

# Chapter 10
## "USING YOUR EBAY AND PAYPAL ACCOUNT"

**FIRST:**
After you receive an email sales conformation in the email account that you used to setup your eBay and PayPal account (etc),

You immediately go to your PayPal account and create an invoice for the product purchase and sale by the customer and send that purchase information by email to the buying customer for proof of purchase, product item processing and then forward records for package tracking in regards to shipping and tracking the package for arrival to the delivery address for your customer.

**IMPORTANT:**
**The policy may have changed by now but..,**
eBay usually will not transfer or release the hold on the funds in your PayPal account until after you have created an invoice within your PayPal account and you have executed sending that invoice to your customer in acknowledgement of the sale to alert your customer for proof of purchase, shipment records and the tracking information of the item purchase shipment.

Once you have done this, eBay will then release the hold on the funds within your PayPal account and you can then proceed with fulfilling the transaction for your customer purchase.

# Chapter 11
## "MAKING MONEY ONLINE IN NO TIME FLAT"

**NEXT:**

#2

After all of the above has been done, immediately go to your suppliers website and using your PayPal business debit card attached to the Paypal account where you have received the payment for the product item that was purchased by your customer, make purchase of the item that was ordered by your customer. At this time during the checkout, alter the shipping information for the product you have ordered with your supplier from that of your own account shipping address to that of your customers so that the product item is shipped to your customers address and not yours.

Alternatively you can call, fax, or email in this change in shipping address for the item(s) you have ordered with your product source company at the time that you make the purchase.

**REMEMBER:**

#3

Use your PayPal debit card and contact your product source company for purchasing the item(s) ordered. Then make purchase of the item(s) for your customers ensuring that the product(s) is being processed for shipping to your end use customer's address. Your source company will then fulfill the order and ship the purchased item(s) to your end use customer address for you.

**(Drop Shipped)**

### DO THIS AND YOU'LL BE MAKING MONEY ONLINE IN NO TIME FLAT!

# Chapter 12
## "HOW TO SET YOUR PROFIT MARGIN"

**NOW.., HOW DO YOU SET YOUR PROFIT MARGIN?**

**FIRST:**
Find the products that you would like to sell.
Try and pick the ones with at least a $150.00 TO $200.00 spread below the MSRV price and preferably with free shipping.

**NEXT:**
#2
Do a quick search for that product online. Try eBay, Amazon, or the like for instance and find the average MSRV sales price.

Once you have done this, begin by setting your profit margin somewhere between the current MSRV product online sell price and the purchase price you pay at your supplier source account.

Remember, with our sources you can find that same product for at least 20% to 50% off the MSRV price.

### AS A RULE OF THUMB:
We recommend that you find and sell products that you can ship for free from the product source list that we provide.

### (USE OUR LIST)
We also recommend that for higher turn over or faster sales you set your profit margin between $20.00 and $60.00 above your total purchase price from your supplier per item at no more or no less.

# Chapter 13
## "WHERE THE MAGIC HAPPENS"

**THIS IS WHERE THE MAGIC HAPPENS!**

Make faster sales when you mark up your product items source cost or price just by only $20.00 to $60.00 of the total amount that you pay to purchase and ship the item to your customer!

This way you can still manage to sell the item at 20% to 50% below the average MSRV price that the item is currently being sold for online and still make a profit. The profit margin here using this technique may be smaller but you do stand to increase the chance to make this profit more often or more frequently. You should also take into account that your profit margin here will vary due to product volume sold as opposed to it's availability as well.

Using this business model you will undercut your competition and beat them to the sale every time!

With ten products per listing and all products sold at least one each at $20 to $60 per item profit, that's a $200.00 TO $600.00 profit margin per day or sales period. Not bad for a days work by all means!

# Chapter 14
## "DO THIS AND MAKE MONEY"

IF YOU REALLY WANT TO MAKE MONEY ONLINE,
We've not only just told you how to do it, but we have also just told you what to do it with as well.

If you want quick access to making money online, use our source list for where to go online and set up your accounts to buy brand new name brand consumer electronics at deeply discounted prices.
If you try doing this yourself it will be a long and very hard search online for a list of product distributors that you can trust with brand new in the box name brand high end electronics that will ship for free every time without fail.

Don't beat yourself treat yourself!

PLEASE USE OUR UNIQUE LIST OF ELECTRONICS SUPPLIERS RIGHT AWAY!

Use our product sources and start making money online within 24-to-72 hours after setting up this easy stupid simple system, and the best part is that you can do it all for free.

If anybody is making money online then this is surely one of the ways they are doing it

**Now we've told you how to do it!**
**Go do it and go make some money doing it!**
**Do this and you will be on your way to making good money using eBay and easily stuffing cash into your PayPal account fast!**

# Chapter 15
## "OUR UNIQUE LIST OF PRODUCT SOURCE COMPANIES"

Okay.., we told you that we would provide you with our unique list of product source companies...,

Well here it is below.

Use this information wisely!

**NOTE AND TIP:**
When posting your ads leave a special marker in the product ad description that only you will recognize to alert you to which product source company you used to source that particular product item when you receive the email sales conformation from PayPal.

**<u>Okay, here's the list!</u>**

http://www.sony.com/dealersource
http://www.samsung.com
http://www.mcmelectronics.com
http://www.megagoods.com
http://www.compuvest.com
http://www.evertek.com
http://www.dell.com
http://www.doba.com

## About the Author

This book was written and published by Morgan W. Johnson Sr. aka MoJohnson Publishing

I have been Internet Network Marketing for over 5 years now, and I'm very well informed in the subject of Affiliate Marketing online. I have sold products on eBay and made money and have decided to share a few secrets with those of like minds to make their incomes from online marketing!

Please enjoy this eBook and to your great success!

### THANKS FOR READING AND YOUR DOWNLOAD!

We would like to think of this as a public service announcement so please enjoy and go make some money!

MOJOHNSON
SPONSORED BY: MAKEMONEYWITHEBAYANDPAYPAL.COM
MoJohnson
Tweet me @MoJohnson36

**Special Offer For You!**

ANOTHER COOL WAY TO MAKE MONEY ONLINE
**GO HERE**
SIGN UP
CREATE YOUR ACCOUNT
AND
MAKE $1.00
EVERYTIME SOMEONE CLICKS ON YOUR LINK TO SIGNUP!
HEY,
**LOYALTE PAYS!**

# Book Description:

### How To Make Money With Your eBay and PayPal Account

This is a much sought after and need to know information mini eBook that explains how make money online using your eBay and PayPal Accounts. With the ongoing loss of jobs not just here in the United State, but around the world more and more people are looking for alternate ways to making an income. This mini-eBook gives a straight to the point very simple way to making money online by selling other peoples products!

### This is a must read for anyone looking to make money online.

With this eBook you will learn to make money with your eBay and PayPal account!

This is not a get rich quick but, it works, and it does make you money!

Read this mini eBook as it will explain how to easily start making money online.

### QUICKLY LEARN HOW IT OPERATES!

This is a quick study buy low and sells high on eBay mini eBook!

Get this short to the point quick page mini eBook and, start making money online with your eBay and PayPal account fast and easy!

If anybody is making money online, this is surely one of the ways that they are doing it!

Use our system and beat your competition to the sell every time!
Make money 48-to-72 hours after setup!

### You don't need your own products!

### You don't need your own website!

### It's not Affiliate Marketing!

### Easy stupid simple system!

### No money to start-up!

### Make faster sales!

Who is this eBook for?
Anyone who wants to make money online!

### READ THIS AND YOU'LL BE MAKING MONEY ONLINE IN NO TIME FLAT!